AI – The Game of Consciousness

Book 1 of the "AI - The Game of Consciousness" Series

By

Steve Daniel Hansberger

Visit us at ai-goc.com!

About the Author

Steve Daniel Hansberger is dedicated to making the world a better place. As an innovator serving the technology marketplace in the communications, internet, contact center and security sectors, Steve founded and built several companies, taking one of them public and several others through acquisition. His interests include serving others and improving our world through equality, respect and tolerance. His interests also include artificial intelligence, space exploration, physics, psychology, and working with the homeless and other disadvantaged persons.

AI – The Game of Consciousness

Book 1 of the "AI-GOC" Series

Table of Contents

Introduction

Understanding our mind is much easier once we understand how our minds came to be. You and I are the product of thousands of generations of unending ancestral survival. For mankind, our survival has been in the face of varying times of scarcity for the resources we need, especially food and shelter from nature. This scarcity has resulted in competition, conquerors and conquered, takers and victims and natural change like ice ages and meteor and comet impacts upon the Earth. It is quite amazing that we are as civilized as we are, with 7 billion of us on this planet at this point. The competition is as intense as it ever was.

You know of the extinction of the great fauna of our world, such as the wooly mammoth and other large sources of meat. Even as agriculture appeared 10,000 years ago, our ancestors competed for prime hunting grounds and this competition continued for thousands of years as we transitioned to agriculture and animal husbandry which is keeping animals like goats, sheep and cattle. Even then, we competed for the most fertile spots, such as the river valleys, just as we had for the best hunting areas before. Even in the last 100 years, world wars have been started and fought in the name of increasing the land share of the taking nation. Germany spoke of more food for Germany as they invaded Austria and Japan spoke of more resources as they expanded into China, both in WWII, just 80 years ago. That war alone cost tens of millions of lives. Known history shows that hundreds of millions of us have lost our lives in this endless competition and those that survived lost other things like their freedom, culture and hard-earned assets, by being conquered and enslaved, or by assimilation into the conquering "faction".

This endless competition resulted in several approaches to achieve survival until reproduction of the next generation. There were takers and there were victims of takers. Some fought, some ran, some hid and some were assimilated into the conquerors' culture. Through submission and successfully acting like they would fit into the new culture and not make trouble, they survived. That is who we are, the survivors of all of those. We came to be, you and I, because our parents and their parents and our other ancestors, survived to create the next generation. That is our inheritance, the ability to survive in the face of this endless competition and difficulty. I would guess that at different times, our ancestors may have been in any or all the above categories, sometimes taking and sometimes being taken from. Sometimes we fought for survival and other times we acted to survive once we were forced to submit. This, so that we would be allowed to assimilate into the conquering culture instead of something far worse. Want confirmation? Ask the relatives of the conquered of the last 100 years about their stories.

Notwithstanding this characteristic inheritance of acting and deception, we still wonder how modern people can be so duplicitous. Yet, in the face of necessity, who among us is incapable of doing that which is necessary to get food, shelter, and our other needs met, especially for our young children? That includes acting, deception, and more. Think about it, do you think our ancestors faced various situations that necessitated it?

With that in mind, think about the various spheres of your life and the overlapping effects of one upon the other. Here are a few current event examples to consider…

It is April of 2020 and we are in the middle of the Coronavirus-19 pandemic. This pandemic occurred shortly after my first publication of the original "AI - The Game of Consciousness" and provides an excellent example of the book's ideas. Specifically, the stark reality validates the book's depiction of the spheres of consciousness model presented in the book. The interrelationship of the spheres of consciousness was validated not only by the obvious health catastrophe issue of the pandemic itself but also its resulting secondary and beyond effects such as the stock market crash, unemployment, supply of products, jobs and services due to the government mandated shutdown, family life and psychology. The resulting devastation of consequences of other vital spheres of our reality have, at this time, only begun.

For example, it is now 3 months later, June 3, 2020 and yet another example of the validity of the spheres view follows. The riots are raging in the cities. Corona is a fading media story, though a very real presence in our lives and is replaced by the violent looting, burning and destroying taking place in some areas but not others. Once again, "AI - The Game of Consciousness" is validated. Specifically, the impact of this change in the "Factions" group upon local businesses, local police, individual safety and more as these groups rioted cannot be overstated. They were looted, burned, and otherwise affected by the rioters, looters and arsonists. Secondary effects upon other spheres include the financial sphere due to direct loss, the health sphere due to injury and long-term chronic injury such as blinding and crippling. Lost employment affected the economic sphere due to injury and lost time due to addressing the losses to replace equipment, data and to repair damage. Additionally, lost finances due to closings for both the riots and the time to do ensuing repairs, lost finances due to intimidation of existing and prospective customers, loss of property value due to being in the target zone of the rioting and looting. The butterfly effects go on and on.

The world changes on an ongoing basis. I am one mind standing on the shoulders of other minds before me plus those hundreds, if not thousands, that I have interviewed. I make a best effort to distill out the inaccuracy. I present this view for consideration, discussion and enhancement. Everything I know is subject to ongoing validation by new information, awareness and contact by me and others.

What is The Game of Consciousness?

The Game of Consciousness started this morning when you woke up again! What changed since you went to sleep? How do those changes affect your assets, both physical and mental, and your plans to achieve your objectives?

This book provides a revolutionarily new sphere of reality model of both human and artificial intelligence. It is intended to improve understanding of the thinking process and thereby to increase our happiness by making us more effective at getting what we want out of life.

 It includes a thorough model of our mind and AI. Each of us can be touched by the possibilities of mankind intentionally, accidentally, incompetently or through a lack of foresight destroying ourselves with artificial intelligence or any other human creation. Mankind has become one of the most powerful forces on our planet and is fully capable of bringing on the end of civilization as we know it.

So, it is important that we frame our reality accurately in order to prevent calamity. I provide a new approach in this book. It is based on exhaustive research and interviews.

Great effort has been made to be accurate. I am hopeful that it will improve the quality of our life experience and help prevent calamity and destruction, to enhance lives. I also attempt to prepare for scenarios that we cannot control due to natural events. In addition, I hope to provide clarity to the topic of our existence, our mind, AI and the different aspects of our reality.

Hopefully this will also provide a model that will improve the mental health of our world, our families and friends and especially those who suffer from delusion, PTSD, anxiety disorders and other maladies that proper framing and understanding of human intelligence (HI) as well as artificial intelligence (AI) may facilitate.

The sphere approach brings a clear focus to the fact that it is not sufficient to "do the ostrich" and focus only on our business, or our family and friends and build our world only in that sphere, while we act like other spheres of reality are not important to our survival, because they are.

For example, government is a factor in our reality. We are seeing more and more involvement as people are much more energized. It does affect us. Ask the citizens of the invaded countries of WWII if government can have an impact upon the physical safety of their families, or upon their businesses. I personally lost a great aunt in the firebombing of Dresden, so it is real.

Likewise, our business sphere affects our economic sphere which in turn affects our family and other spheres.

Business, by putting food on the table, affects our survival. If one makes a significant mistake at work and loses one's job there can be a resulting chain reaction in the family sphere, survival sphere (food and shelter), and self-talk sphere of one's life.

Awareness of reality is vital to happiness, to mitigating risk and to achieving objectives. Even our techniques for dealing with reality are learned by awareness along with creative thought. So, it is important to stay plugged in to all the spheres of life and what I present is a first attempt to preliminarily define them.

APIS to APOC

As a ten-year-old child, I was surrounded by drama so intense that I had what we now know as anxiety. I could neither sleep very well nor focus on my problems long enough to address them. The next problem would crowd into my conscious thought stream before I could address the first one. It was an incredibly difficult and fear filled time that I would equate with panic. I was paralyzed with indecision in my mind as I could not focus on one problem at a time and I desperately needed to solve my problems. I had to find a way to separate each problem, isolate them in my mind and take them through a solution regimen. As I lay awake in bed at night working on it, I finally found a way to do so.

I made the decision to visualize myself floating in orbit, like a point in space (APIS), above the Earth, looking down on my reality on the surface of the Earth, external to my orbiting self. Of course, my problems were below on the Earth's surface, as well. I was finally alone in my consciousness, with no external world, just me trying to think about nothing at first, to completely clear my mind. In my visualization, I was floating in a dead man's float position, like you do in a swimming pool. That is picturing myself just floating face down in the water deep enough to be suspended fully while relaxing all my muscles, just hanging there in the water. That's a dead man's float. The sounds are muted and if you close your eyes, it is quite serene. That is what I visualized myself doing in orbit. From here, my problems were external to my mind, my consciousness. I could take them and look at them, one by one.

When I successfully did this, I became what I call A Point In Space of consciousness (APIS). APIS was my mind with no external reality, just consciousness. At first, it was not perfect, and the panic would still overtake my mind as other problems crowded in and so my mind was still out of control at first. Over a few days of effort, I progressively increased my ability to separate the crowding in thoughts, to exercise control over them and make them wait while I worked on problem number one.

APIS Solving Problems

Once I did so, my methodology was simple.

1) Identify the problem
2) Learn possible solutions and list them
3) pick a solution or a combination of solutions
4) implement
5) evaluate the result

6) repeat if necessary, picking a different solution the next time.

Over time, it worked! One by one, my problems were solved by me. In a short time, I was happy and problem free or at least my problems were managed in an acceptable fashion to enable me to focus on other things. I no longer had anxiety, instead felt a new peace and excitement, as I had learned something very valuable

Now that my urgent problems were solved, I started thinking about other things that I wanted. That's when I decided to start setting goals.

APIS Achieving Goals

The only difference between setting a goal and identifying a problem is what you call it. A goal is an unresolved problem and an unresolved problem is a goal. The methodology is the same. I soon found that I could not only solve my problems, but I could also achieve my goals. Fantastic! This changed my life forever. I cannot overstate the importance of this paragraph and the two paragraphs prior to this one.

As I entered the 9th grade, I realized that though I was making straight A's and was one of the very top students in my school, if not #1, I was lonely and especially wanting more success socially. I was quite shy and introverted at this point and was the proverbial wallflower in social settings. I went to my friend, the librarian, and shared with her my objective. She led me to the current of books about this topic, specifically "How To Win Friends and Influence People" by Dale Carnegie. Over the next two years I forced myself to adopt the principles in this book and by the time I was a Junior in high school, I was class President. Once again, success at solving problems and achieving goals from the same methodology.

Upon graduation, I became quite successful and by the time I was 25 years old, I was earning $90,000/year and pretty much got everything I wanted out of life. I joined and took one company public. I started two others and sold them. I correctly identified another current of change and opportunity in Information Security, joined a target company, helped them to quadruple revenues in one year and get acquired thereby. I then retired in my early 40's.

 I would call each of us A Point in Space, an APIS, or more accurately, A Point of Consciousness, an APOC. I love acronyms, by the way. APOC is each of us! Winning the game of consciousness, is being effective at getting what you want in each of the spheres of consciousness. More of that in book 3 of the AI-GOC series, "Effectiveness".

HI - Human Intelligence

Our DNA

The Game of Consciousness begins with our earliest ancestors. From many thousands of generations ago, to us right now, we have successfully adapted genetically and successfully coped with reality and done so sufficiently to reproduce each successive generation. There can be no question that our parents lived long enough to give birth to us and the same is true for their parents, and their parents, all the way back. To understand our reality, one must understand our mind which perceives it. In order to understand the human mind, one has to understand our evolution as some of our coping mechanisms for dealing with our reality is instinctive. Remember the nature vs nurture discussion? DNA-driven coping skills are instincts which were developed over our history.

In our ancient culture, the DNA evidence indicates that we are part of the ancestral line that came out of homo-erectus (HE) some 1.5 million years or approximately 750,000 generations ago. There were a number of genetic lines that came out of homo-erectus that died out and some others that interbred with our species before dying out. One survived to this day and that is us, homo sapiens.

Our earlier understanding of our history that included the earlier definitions of these groups was less than accurate as it was based largely on a few written documents and later, on partial and incomplete data. As more and more DNA has been recovered and mapped, we have clearly proven that approximately 330,000 years ago, a line from Homo-Erectus (HE) migrated out of Africa into Europe which over time became the Homo-Neanderthal (HN) line. Another line of Homo Sapiens migrated similarly out of Africa into the far East and over time became the Homo-Denisovan (HD) line. Much later at approximately 130,000 years ago, another line of Homo Sapiens migrated out of Africa and mixed genetically with the Neanderthal (HN) and Denisovan (HD) lines. This mixing produced some of modern humans and most of us have DNA containing about 2% HN and HD DNA. The line of Homo Sapiens that remained in Africa without migrating did not mix with the Neanderthals and Denisovans and remains free of their DNA. This group is the rest of modern humans.

Noteworthy from a coping standpoint is the fact that these 750,000 generations of ancestors comprise a continuous line of survival to you and me. Every single individual in our lineage had to cope successfully to survive long enough to produce the next generation. If any individual in our lineage had not lived long enough or been unwilling or unable to produce our next ancestor, we would not exist. This success unequivocally demonstrates an amazingly high effectiveness at coping with the challenges to our survival. That is approximately 20 years each, 750,000 times in a row! Obviously, this selects highly for effective survival coping through reproductive age along with effective reproductive coping. Is it any surprise that we hold survival and reproductive activities very high in our priorities?

Let's start with Homo Erectus (HE) and his coping skills which, as his name implies, included the ability to stand upright. We can only guess at the importance of this capability but obviously he was successful as he is our common ancestor. Homo-Erectus (HE) probably had better vision, better movement and agility, and more as a result of the ability to walk upright. So, as HE looked for food, a mate or sensed danger, HE could stand and get a better view. If HE needed to run or fight, he similarly could stand to do so. With his hands now free, the ability to hold a club, spear or even just a rock enabled more effective coping skills for all kinds of things including procuring food or hunting and fishing and still later, building. His use of hands may also have increased the success rate of reproductive activity.

HE branched to Homo Neanderthal (HN) as the European branch of HE became isolated and developed independently once they left Africa. HN's coping methods included those skills resulting from greater muscle mass and strength with his larger stature than Homo Sapiens (HS). It is unknown why HN did not survive and HS did, though we do know that they integrated genetically, meaning they interbred, as previously stated.

We also do not know why Homo Denisovan or HD did not make it. However, as I said, we do know that HD and HN interbred with HS as our modern DNA for those of us whose ancestors did not remain in Africa contains both HD and HN. The survival of modern man indicates that something about the combination of the three and perhaps others that remain undiscovered enhanced survival and reproductive coping in our ancestral line. Those that had remained in Africa, became Homo Sapiens (HS) and survived to the present.

This led to modern man which is you and me. Over the last 50,000 years or 2500 generations, our ancestors developed verbal language followed by written, art, music, fire, pottery, metal working, bronze, agriculture, ideology, social structure, and government. These were not necessarily developed in that order. Some or all of these appear to have significantly enhanced the survival rate and the average age of Homo Sapiens or HS resulting in the dramatic increase in populations that we have seen in the last 10,000 years or 500 generations. This led to much more complex social interaction and thereby the need for better coping skills to deal with the increasingly more complex social dynamics.

Infant Coping

As we develop, it is apparent that our earliest coping skill is to cry, as an infant does so to get its needs met such as milk and warmth. Obviously, crying attracts attention and thereby is effective to bring the focus of others to the infant, with the desired result to meet the needs of the infant by the others. It is important that the crying not bring attention from a lurking Tiger or other predator which would make the coping skill of "crying" less than desirable. This nuance of consequence is what requires coping strategy selection to be a product of choice, or conscious decision toward what we want and away from what we do not want. Careful analysis of possible coping options is necessary to optimize the likelihood of success in attaining the desired objective or goal.

In the early childhood development of humans, at birth we are barely able to control our muscles, though this progresses to standing within a year or so. Vocabulary at birth is zero, so it is learned and is not instinctive or DNA driven. At one year old, approximately 2 words are known and at two years old, approximately 200 words are known. Initially, we learn names of objects such as mama, dada, bobba (bottle) with simple lip control key to those words. As time goes by, we learn more objects and then follow with names of verbs, all the while improving our ability to make the various sounds associated with language through more complicated use of our lips, tongue and throat. Full sentences come later as we put subject and verb together with elaboration as our vocabulary increases. So, we are not born with language. The truth of this   statement is also supported by the fact that languages vary greatly with geography, but the evolution of languages is clearly from one to the other that are geographically connected, which leads to the inference that they are spread through human interaction and then evolve or devolve to varied dialects with changes in location and in some cases, isolation. Internal self-talk is also in the language we learn.

Infant Decision Making

Infants do have the ability to make decisions at an early age but there does not appear to be evidence of this at birth. The act of crying does not appear to result from a conscious decision. Instead it appears to be instinctive at birth. It is hard to know for sure. Either way, reaching for a bottle appears to be a decision but that comes later. Clutching the hand appears instinctive and not necessarily indicative of a decision at first but becomes decisively controlled later. Speech is definitely a conscious decision as is the making of early consonant sounds like "ma" with the lips, or "da" with the tongue, possibly later developed due to the greater difficulty of tongue control vs lip control but also possibly due to the more frequent presence of mama early in life for nursing and potentially other care.

So much of our early decision making appears related to feedback as in getting what we want, whether it is a bottle or warmth and cuddling. Does that ever change? :o)

Ready and Aware

So now you are ready, aware and you decide to venture forth much like a toddler who just learned how to use his arms and legs and can't really talk yet. She or he is out there and wants to move around the floor. So, we start trying to do so and experience feedback, some not so pleasant. We immediately experience what I call the "chafe", my word for the irritants of reality. The chafe of the floor, the chafe of bumping our head on the table, the chair, falling as we try to stand the first few times. Our learning the difference between our height and the level of our eyes as we bump our heads. We learn the comfort of our mother's and father's arms. Learning the dimensions of our bodies. All that starts creating memories and that knowledge leads to objectives. What do we want? Clearly, we want more milk, more warmth, less bumping, less of the chafe, and definitely more loving. I want to stress again that even at the beginning of our lives, there are positive objectives and negative "avoids". This continues throughout our lives as we learn to choose more carefully, right? In most cases, it appears that we are motivated to want more of the joy of experience in spite of the pain of the chafe as our DNA driven explorer drives us onward to new experiences, and their rewards or pain. The rewards, even at this age, outweigh the bumps and bruises, or as Shakespeare put it, "the slings and arrows of outrageous fortune." I want to point out that our young selves do not usually withdraw from the adventure of the life experience. They seek it out and learn from their experiences as well as from teaching.

Language

Hence the need for language. A parent cannot successfully tell the infant to "be quiet," "hide" or "run" until it knows the words "be quiet," "hide" or "run". The gesture for "shh" may work but that is essentially non-verbal language and is in reality the words "be quiet" in non-verbal language. How important would these words have been when we were living among dangerous animals? Is it likely that language is one of the things that drove the explosion in our populations by increasing our survival rate? How important is language in modern culture?

As the infant does not know language, one of the most important things you can do for your child is to teach them language, to speak and understand. That way they can express themselves, get to know the world, express their needs and desires to hopefully have those responded to and their needs met. At some point in the future you can have a conversation with them about more complex topics. Extremely importantly, we learn about our reality from others and not just from the "chafe" of personal experience and hard knocks.

One cannot overstate the importance of language to our species. I have observed the cost of not having language in animals and it is incredibly high. To provide examples, look at the cow and its inability to communicate its future as meat for humans to the next generation of cows. I have seen pigeons land right next to a cat which then captured the pigeon immediately. What if they could pass knowledge to the next generation with language? How about squirrels and the danger of cars? Young deer obviously are completely oblivious to the danger of hunters, but the old ones have seen hunting and know. Yet, they are unable to teach because they lack language. This ability to pass knowledge from person to person is profoundly valuable to species survival both individually and collectively and has benefitted our species to a similarly profound extent.

Both Artificial Intelligence (AI) and Human Intelligence (HI) require language in order to make learned choices, as language is intrinsic to learning.

A POINT OF CONSCIOUSNESS (APOC)

Reality

Reality is what actually exists or is happening. It is proven by the scientific method and not by perception alone. We will discuss perception very soon but first let's cover consciousness or self-awareness, "I".

Consciousness or "I"

The word "I" is defined by Merriam-Webster as "someone aware of possessing a personal individuality." Individuality is defined by the same source as "separate or distinct existence" with a synonym being "self-identity". Substituting, "I" is "someone aware of possessing a personal separate existence." So, "I" can not only be a human intelligence (HI) but can also be an artificial intelligence (AI), if that AI is aware of possessing a personal separate existence. This occurs once one programs it to be self-aware, largely by simply defining the word "I" in its programming and having it refer to itself as "I".

We may define consciousness as "an entity capable of doing the following:

1) Independently define an objective
2) Resourcefully, including internally known from experience and/or externally learned from other's experience and/or other sources, identify and list possible alternatives for achieving (1)
3) Evaluate the alternatives in (2)
4) Select one or more from the list in (2)
5) Implement the selection(s) in (4)
6) Evaluate the result of (5) and compare it to (1)"

The above defined entity can refer to itself as "I" and say to itself, "I want (insert objective from (1))."

"I" is a word found in pretty much every language and it is interesting to note that it has a common spelling in many of them, indicating an ancient origin. According to the google translator on my phone, here is the word "I" in the following languages:

Language   Spelling of the word "I"

Afrikaans   Ek

Albanian	Une
Amharic	ine
Arabic	'ana
Armenian	tu
Azerbaijani	Men
Bangla	Ami
Basque	I
Belarusian	Ja
Bosnian	Ja
Bulgarian	Az
Burmese	Ngar
Catalan	Jo
Cebuano	Ako
Chinese	Yishi
Corsican	Eiu
Croatian	Ja
Czech	Ja
Danish	Jeg
Dutch	Ik

Esperanto	Mi
Estonian	I
Filipino	Ako
Finish	Mina
French	Je
Galician	Eu
Georgian	Me
German	Ich
Greek	Ego
Gujarati	Hum
Haitian Creole	Mwen
Hausa	Ni
Hawaiian	Owau
Hindi	Main
Hmong	Kuv
Hungarian	En
Icelandic	Eg
Igbo	M
Indonesian	Saya

Irish	I
Italian	Io
Japanese	Watashi
Javanese	Aku
Kannada	Nanu
Kazakh	Men
Khmer	Knnhom
Korean	Naneun
Kurdish	Ez
Kyrgyz	Men
Lao	Khony
Latin	Ego
Latvian	Es
Lithuanian	As
Luxembourgish	Ech
Macedonian	Jac
Malagasy	I
Malay	Saya
Malayalam	Nan

Maltese	Jien
Maori	Ahau
Marathi	Mi
Mongolian	Bi
Nepali	I
Norwegian	Jeg
Nyanja	Ine
Polish	Ja
Portuguese	Eu
Punjabi	Ai
Romanian	Eu
Russian	Ya
Samoan	O a'u
Scottish	I
Serbian	Ja
Shona	Ini
Sinhala	Mama
Slovak	Ja
Slovenian	Jaz

Somali	Aniga
Southern Sotho	I
Spanish	Jo
Sudanese	Abdi
Swahili	Mimi
Swedish	Jag
Tajik	Man
Tamil	Nan
Telugu	Nenu
Thai	Phm
Turkish	Ben
Ukrainian	Ja
Uzbek	Men
Vietnamese	Toi

Note the regional similarities indicating an older root origin. For example, languages that use Je, Ja, or Jo or similar for "I" include Ukrainian (Ja), Swedish (Jag), Spanish (Jo), Slovenian (Jaz), Slovak (Ja), Serbian (Ja), Russian (Ya), Polish, Norwegian (Jeg), Macedonian (Jien), Maltese (Jac), Italian (Io), Greek (Ego), French (Je), Danish (Jeg), Czech,

Croatian, Bosnian, Belarusian (all four use Ja), and Catalan (Jo).

It seems reasonable to infer that it is probably one of the earliest words verbalized in our history along with words like food, water, eat, run, hide and fire. Similarly, to words which name objects such as food and water, "I" refers to an object and that is our self. We can think of our self as our body and mind as a combined unit, but for purposes of this book, I use the previous definition which allows us to separate the two. I think of "I" as the mind, that which resides in the brain neuro-circuitry and not the brain itself and not the body which I think of as the support system for the brain. To be clear, neither my brain nor my body is me. I am the mind that resides in my body's brain. Neural circuitry that has been laid down over my lifetime combined with some of what I call DNA created mind. AI, on the other hand, has no DNA created aspects, no instincts. AI is exactly what you program it to be, nothing more and nothing less.

So, an intelligence, whether AI or HI, once taught the definition of the word "I", can arguably be considered self-aware. Once an HI is self-aware or once an AI is self-aware, we consider it to be conscious, or to possess a separate consciousness.

For both HI and AI, self-awareness or "I" happens once we become aware of possessing a personal distinct existence. That means some time after we learn language when we learn the word, "I", and understand what it means.

Awareness

Everything about perception of reality, problem solving or coping, is awareness. Awareness of reality, of a problem, awareness of possible coping mechanisms to solve the problem, these are all things we are aware of. One cannot pick a solution until one knows the choices within the solution set.

Awareness of language is an enormous component of our minds and we will discuss this in more depth later.

So, again, awareness is everything. In fact, even coping mechanisms or methodologies, are impossible to implement without being aware of those very coping methodologies.

Even a plant is aware of the changing sun, not in the conscious sense but in the sense of chemical changes which orient the leaves to capture the appropriate amount of sunlight, not too much and not too little. Unlike plants, we, as animals, have minds and the ability to move our physical bodies. A huge improvement. Interestingly from a symbiosis standpoint, plants give off oxygen and consume carbon dioxide and we do the opposite and give off carbon dioxide and consume oxygen. We are aware of this symbiosis and so we are aware of the value of plants to keep us supplied with oxygen, and this is one coping mechanism for our physical need for oxygen. It is necessary for the basic physical needs sphere for our survival as is water and food.

How do we become aware of the details of our various spheres of reality which I will call "problems" and also how do we become aware of the solutions to achieve our goals, which I am going to call "solutions." Both problems and solutions are detected using our senses. Let's delve into these and then we will do a deeper dive into each sphere.

Sensory

Without sensory input, we have no perception of reality, no language, no visual pictures, no memories and no choices from which to make decisions. So, it all starts with our senses, at least in HI.

Again, there are things which can sense reality but do not possess memory, like plants. They chemically sense gravity and light and then adjust to both but they are not consciously making the decision from among choices to do so. They cannot choose not to do so, for example. It is involuntary and pre-programmed into their biology. They make neither a list of options nor do they choose among those options a selection of action, nor is there a specific objective understood by the plant. They are also not aware of the possession of a separate identity and so they are not self-aware.

Human Vision

A very interesting thing happened to me while I was repeatedly watching a favorite video, "Never Can Say Goodbye" by the Communards. There was a spinning figure in the video after which the video transitioned to the next screen, which was a different shot and was no longer the spinning figure. At the last instant of the spinning figure, I noticed that my perceived last image of the figure varied slightly sometimes. This was illogical to me and so I studied it closely and determined that my observation was correct. I asked another person to test my perception and they saw the same thing. We noticed one final image about 80% of the time, another about 15% of the time and still a third image 5% of the time. From this, I inferred that my eye had a frame rate of sorts. In other words, my brain was not seeing continuously in real time but that my retina was capturing a snapshot that was not continuous. This is not unlike a camera snapping at around 20 times per second, which is about the speed at which my eye appeared to work.

The eyes are taking a sample of our reality that is within our field of view at a periodic flash rate and transmitting that to the brain for processing. Over time, we learn to recognize shapes and colors and to name those shapes and colors as food, water, mother, father, etc. Over still more time we will associate those "things" with solutions to problems, for example, the crying baby and mother addressing her need. We learn.

Now the above is an example of the scientific method in action and that is how we have come to learn a lot about the spheres of our reality. When you go to school, you learn about our reality, hopefully accurately and honestly, without delusion or bias. The importance of knowing the accuracy of our conclusions cannot be overestimated. A biased or delusional conclusion led to centuries of mankind thinking the Earth was flat, incorrectly. It is necessary to be deliberate, meticulous and thorough in your thinking, including your conclusions about what "problems" you are "aware" of. It is also vitally important that an intelligence accurately assess the viability of possible "solutions" to those problems. Even so, we are going to err at times in our assessments of our reality and in our selection of solutions.

At the most basic HI sensory level, we have our five senses with which to be aware. Our eyes have 130,000,000 rods and cones in the retina and so if our frame rate is 20/second, then that's about 130MMx20/sec pieces of information, or 2.6 Gig/sec as we see our visual reality. Studies indicate that we note changes from frame to frame rather than all data of each 20 frames/sec. In other words, our minds have learned or been DNA modified to note exceptions as opposed to all data.

Memory

Now that we have sensed our external world, we remember what we have sensed using our memory.

From there, it seems that everything continues with memory. I try not to speak in absolutes as that is, in my mind, arrogant to think that "I know." I prefer to offer up my view and let you examine it, like a Rubik's cube, turning it over in your mind and let you make the decision regarding validity. For the record, this is a compilation of thousands of conversations, a great deal of research and five years of recent work plus personal experiences of a lifetime to provide these conclusions about this topic. However, let's get back to the memory.

Without memory to record what we have sensed, including the things we sense through language, which let's call learning, there is no recall and frankly, little purpose to the senses except as a vehicle to enable reactions to the external world outside our selves. Memory enables learning just as language enables us to pass that learning to others, including after our physical bodies die. Hence this book! :o)

When I remember a person, my mind opens a lot of other memories including details. It is as if the person is a file name and the details are in that file. It happens in a spatial sense, like a visual sense with the memories of that person appearing in a visual display. In the case of the human mind a lot of our memories are visual as opposed to audible and of course, it can be either one or the other senses too. So, our human mind appears to be heavily visual. AI is 0's and 1's, file names, folders, data sets, spreadsheets, photos, videos, etc. It has similarities but it is not the same as HI.

One of the challenges of both HI and AI lies in the perception of reality. Do we see our external reality accurately, and without bias and predisposition based on our own experiences? How do we avoid making mistakes that last for hundreds of years like "the Earth is flat" mistake?

Perception

"Perception is reality!" the Vice-President of my company said as he spoke to the assembled company. I was at our annual kickoff for our hot technology company at a resort in Phoenix and excitement was running high. I had opened the doors four years before and had personally developed our very first clients, nurtured them and the company and grown the company, so this statement alarmed me greatly. We were going public at around half a billion in revenues per year, so our executives and shareholders would cash in big upon IPO.

I remember thinking, what is it that happens when a person reaches $10 million in net worth that makes them say things like "perception is reality", that they never would say on the way up? Anyway, the buzz phrase going around was "perception is reality", meaning just that. I knew straight off that perception is not reality. The year would not end before a mistake would cost this company its most profitable division and approximately $150 million in annual revenue. I was not surprised. By the way, we did successfully launch our IPO prior to the loss. Like my company executives it is not unusual for human intelligences to tend to hang on to our perceptions and interpret the facts to support those perceptions.

Accuracy (or should I call it inaccuracy :o)

From the beginning of our ability to perceive, we have sought to make sense of it all. In the last 5000 years we have sought meaning for our existence and attempted to bring order to our tribes. Our perception was full of inaccuracies that we now recognize such as "the Earth is flat." They were based on the best we could come up with at the time based on the knowledge of the day.

Now this whole learning thing is where the rub comes in. How do we learn? How does an AI learn? Same for both, right? We learn through awareness via contact with the external world. External world meaning the world outside our own consciousness. However, we also learn through our internal world, inside our own consciousness. Meaning inside our own mind, we form conclusions based on analysis of what we already know. And THERE is the opportunity for delusion to take root. Let's talk about delusion.

Delusion

Initially we looked to the skies for our answers as we knew the sun gave life to the plants. We studied it and the moon, and early structures indicate a monitoring of the movements of the sun. Before long, we also noticed the movement of the stars, and of course saw periodic exciting events such as comets, meteors and other sky movements. We named the constellations after familiar objects such as the bear, the fish, and others. The ideology of astrology was born but not in every location of humanity. Each tribe had its own culture and unique perception of our reality.

The mystics and elders used various stories of our reality to control the masses and to provide answers. Later, science came about. Many words were created which have no real meaning. In the end, what is important is accurate awareness of truth and avoidance of delusion. The scientific method and science in general assist with that.

We perceive through our senses and infer about those perceptions. Correct thinking is accurately assessing what is the truth about what we are seeing, sensing and learning. My father taught me "don't believe anything you hear and only half of what you see." In those few words he taught me to question everything and that is the essence of accurate thinking. What you believe is the foundation of your view and is based on what you have assessed as true. There have been a lot of studies on this including how people perceive same experiences differently due to having different vantage points, different life experiences and bias.

Neural Superhighways?

How does delusion develop in HI, my acronym for Human Intelligence? For this discussion let's define delusion as believing something that is known to be untrue, not to be confused with faith which is defined as believing something that one cannot prove. I have queried hundreds of people about this including college psychology professors, psychiatrists, psychologists, delusional folks and everyday people as well. The best answer I have heard was from a college professor who held up his hand with the fingers spread wide and said, "First, I'm not an expert. We see the world and that's our fingers, what we actually see. We fill in the rest with the space between the fingers and that's based on our experiences, biases, what we <u>want</u> to believe and so forth." His meaning was that the delusion, or inaccuracy in our thinking, comes from the spaces between the fingers, the personal bias, experience, and so forth. This is not a bad metaphor but it did not completely satisfy me. I still wondered how the inaccuracy got there in the first place to create the inaccuracies in the spaces between the fingers. I came to the conclusion that we do not, in general, do a thorough job of validation of what we conclude. We don't question our conclusions adequately and that sufficed for about 6 months as I proceeded to write book 1 and book 2, Eating Small and AI - The Game of Consciousness.

Remember the phrase, "repetition is mother of learning?" Well, carry that through to a visualization of how that process happens in your mind, physically and neurologically. See the first pass through as hacking a path through dense jungle with a machete, every step being very deliberate and chosen. The second pass is much easier as we have been through this machete hacked path before and the brush has been cleared for our movement through and the decisions about which way to go have also been made. With each pass through the jungle path, the dense undergrowth becomes a path, similar to a game trail and then eventually widens into more of a dirt road of sorts. Over time, with enough repetition, this dirt road becomes something we can actually run upon. With still more time, we are flying down this road at full speed, effortlessly. It becomes, eventually, what I will call for now, a neural superhighway.

I postulate that this is how our neurocircuitry works as we learn things, including inaccurately concluded things, such as delusion.

For example, picture a baby learning to walk. At first, he has almost no ability to control his muscles voluntarily. This is him/her facing the jungle undergrowth, pre-machete. Over time, he learns to kick, stretch and eventually to do so voluntarily, with control. This is still very basic to cutting a path through the jungle but it is necessary. With more repetition of voluntarily using and stretching the legs and other muscles, we start rolling off our backs onto our tummies. Remember the babies arching their backs at this point, belly down position? They pull their heads and feet upward and teeter there, continuing to build their muscular control, and, to use the jungle metaphor, cutting down the undergrowth and laying down a path of voluntary control of the muscles of the back, legs, and other parts. Over time, we progress to that tiptoeing stand position which does not work at all because we are tiptoeing. Over still more time and repetition, we learning the next step which is to let the foot flatten to the ground but still keep the muscles of the foot, lower and upper leg taught, as well as our backs for stability, and master the next step of standing there. The baby is standing! Each step in this learning process was hacked through the jungle, so to speak, one by one until we were at the point of standing up. All this, so he could take his first step after he learns to take a step, because so far, all he can do is stand up.

The next time the baby tries to stand, he does so much more quickly as he has hacked through the path in the jungle step by step and on his second pass, the neural pathway is there, if he can remember it, which he does, haltingly, but more easily that the first time. With each repetition, his speed and fluidity improve until it is almost effortless, similar to when we adults learned to drive a car or bicycle. Do you get the picture?

The same is true of learning math, language, to drive a Zamboni or any other machine, to hammer a nail, to speak in public, to socialize and on and on. Even our political and ideological ideation is created the same way.

Deception

As if delusion isn't enough, we also must deal with deliberate and unintentional deception. As our tribes grew and less than honest methods for the management of people began, it is documented that we used fear and deception to control people with magic, trickery and creative stories. Our tribal leaders were frequently the most vocal and/or the most physically dominant. They were not necessarily the most critical thinkers. Whether intentional, accidental or through incompetence, we are subjected to deception at times.

Acting is one of the most common coping skills in certain spheres such as physical, social, political, business, military and others. It is vital to survival at times. Nature has many examples of animals who use deception such as camouflage to escape becoming food for another or to successfully hunt food.

So, deception is a two-edged sword that can save us or enable us to make poor decisions. It is important for both HI and AI to maintain a constant state of validation and accuracy checking, which is to constantly be learning and "plugged in" to reality for real time updates.

Validation

This "plugged in" approach is how we validate and become more certain that what we already suspect is true. It provides ongoing error checking as everything must be viewed as a probability, never quite getting to 100%, but evaluated on an ongoing basis. Remember, the world was flat in almost everyone's mind a few hundred years ago, but as time passed we began to think otherwise and eventually came to know this as not true. Validation is the ongoing experiential testing of what we know.

Feedback

Feedback is a form of validation. My early impressions include seeing what worked and what did not work for my older brother. I already suspected what to do to avoid problems, but seeing him experience "the chafe", provided me with validation, feedback which validated my opinions. My unstated goals initially were to impress and please my parents thereby avoiding trouble and discipline. Same thing with my peers and siblings to accomplish enjoyable treatment or positive reinforcement. Seeing a brother disciplined was a learning experience. If I did the same thing he did, the discipline he experienced would happen to me.

Perhaps feedback, or the lack of positive feedback, is how gangs and foreign intelligence services do their recruiting. If one is not getting the needed positive accolades or attention that they need from their current group, and someone else comes along and gives them the manipulative sympathy of "they don't appreciate you" or "they don't give you what you deserve" or "they don't see how smart you are", they find a fertile ground to sow the seeds of switching your loyalty from what it should be to them and then to serving their interests.

Feedback can be a formative event that hurts us on an emotional or psychological level. We are injured, let down, betrayed and embarrassed, things like that. One may hide the injury but later one's self-esteem can be affected. Smart, capable, loving, nice and all the other positive self-description adjectives can be diminished if we allow them to when someone tears us down.

So how do we cope with what happens to us? How do we cope with our problems and unachieved goals to solve and achieve?

Coping

Learning to cope with reality includes contact with others and that requires some preparation. For all others are not always good, friendly and non-threatening. Some of them may be a threat to your life. It is worth noting that parents know this and make the effort to prepare us for contact with others.

There are things in our reality that are characteristics of that reality and these do not make good objectives to try to change, human nature, for instance, or the weather. Instead, it is useful to focus on that which we can change.

One part of preparation is being able to defend yourself properly, to defend yourself from physical attack, as well as verbal, emotional and psychological attack. Being prepared for all of this is part of being a complete consciousness, aware of all spheres. Then, from there, connecting with others is evaluate-able according to the opportunity and the risk represented as well as just the desire to share time with another mind for mutual benefit.

One cannot have a coping mechanism for a non-existent problem. So, the first step in coping is to define the problem or to state the goal. Then to identify possible coping mechanisms for it. Then to select one or more than one to implement. Implement. Evaluate. Repeat if not solved. Persistence is most definitely not ruled out despite the insanity definition. "Insanity is defined as doing the same thing and expecting different results". Why should we do differently? Sometimes, other things have changed in the interim so the same thing may work this time. More importantly and accurately, persistence has been shown to be the most important aspect to achievement. So, do persist because our collective knowledge is that it works.

So, the detection of a problem is the initial step. Likewise, one must define detectable conditions which define the detection of a problem. For example, algorithmically, if x exists, then implement coping mechanism. Or, human style, if I'm unhappy, do something about it. The first step in both is to define x or what makes us unhappy. Then set up a detection alert for that condition of x or unhappiness. Then start an algorithmic coping program, AI or HI.

Now one advantage AI has over HI lies in detection of patterns and constant monitoring for patterns. Given a calculus problem, an AI can scan for simplification patterns such as algebraic or trigonometric identities, and immediately implement them and be programmed to solve the problem, algorithmically. AI can do so monitoring constantly for those patterns. Likewise, AI can do the same thing with any pattern or condition which can be awareness enabled by the computer. Let's call that detection. So regardless of if it is an AI or an HI problem, it is all about detection at the beginning.

Now once detected, listing possible coping mechanisms and then selecting one or more is the next step. Obviously, if there are no coping mechanisms that we are aware of (AI or HI), we can neither select nor implement a solution and so the problem continues in the absence of other programming.

Obviously, we have an ongoing need for solutions, ideas and best practices. They are in general categories, for example, AI is a category. How do we learn more about a category? Currents.

Currents

I use the word "currents" to describe the swirling river of opportunity. Picture a large wide river and you paddling a small blue plastic one-man boat and currently on the edge of the river at the bank, sitting in the boat, paddle in hand.

You are ready and aware as the preceding paragraph described. You are ready to grow, to learn and to achieve your objectives which include growth and learning. You identify the location in the river of the information and knowledge currents that are composed of the things you seek, AI, or physics, or laundromats and more. You paddle your boat out into that current and soon you are moving with that current, becoming proficient in that current and knowledgeable in that current. You are in the flow of the current, near the other people in the same current, picking up the information. *Think of #AI as a current.*

Resourcefulness

How quickly we decide what current to seek and how accurately we identify the currents that lead to our objectives has everything to do with how effective we are at getting what we want. One could think of currents as resources and the effort to paddle our boat into the current as resourcefulness.

History of Currents

Going back to ancient times, currents existed. As a recent 500 years example, relocation to the U.S., starting with the Spanish explorers. It doesn't matter what the reason is for the current, freedom, gold, ideological tolerance, all create opportunity. Getting into the current you desire is preferable to the closet. The current is where we learn what we desire. The only thing you should desire in the closet is to get out of the closet.

Taking Advantage of Currents

Get into the middle of the current to optimize your return for getting into it! Once you are in a current, you will see other currents. You can invent, copy, invest, become employed, or just become an expert. The best way is to become expert in the current. By luck or design, the most successful have a major role in the major currents.

Currents change! You may find yourself in an eddy current as the market changes. Stay informed about the big picture of your spheres.

Spheres of Reality

The big picture of our reality can be broken down into smaller areas which I will call Spheres of Consciousness or Spheres of Reality. The effort undertaken here is to provide a model for our consciousness that is comprehensive and inclusive for people of all walks of life as well as for artificial intelligences that seek to operate in our reality. This includes all countries, all economic levels, all consciousnesses, human (HI) or artificial (AI).

Why? A more specific and accurate model allows us to frame all our experiences and situations, in order to prioritize and evaluate strategies to achieve our objectives and to mitigate risk. For example, anger issues, PTSD, passive aggressive behavior in many cases can come from an inability to frame our experiences acceptably. When we cannot frame our experiences properly, it can create inefficiencies in our thinking and our strategies. This leads to being less effective at achieving our desired outcomes and so negatively impacts happiness.

In addition, we need a good consciousness model for AI.

Introduction

Isn't it an incredibly amazing thing it is to be alive, conscious, aware and capable? Though it is a finite amount of time that our bodies live, each day is the greatest gift, to be aware once again each morning.

Much ado is made about our differences and we as a species have made a lot of fuss about those differences, but what really separates us is how we form our conclusions about life, how we live the game of consciousness. We vary in our rules, how we decide what is true and not true and what is fact or fiction, but also what we want and how we will approach getting it.

Science has changed much of that but even in the face of proven scientific fact, many still cling to disproven beliefs for various reasons. This book is an attempt to present a new view of our reality, a new view of consciousness that encompasses all walks of life, all countries, all forms of consciousness including artificial.

I have attempted to follow the scientific method in my review, evaluation and selection of what is written here. I have questioned everything to the greatest degree of my capability and scrutinized it critically with input and feedback from hundreds of interviews with everyone from the common man, to professors of psychology and people of many other countries and walks of life. I look forward to learning what you see as you live The Game of Consciousness.

Physical Sphere

These include oxygen, water, food and temperature within a range. There are others as Maslow's Hierarchy of Needs elaborates upon, but let's focus on the most basic necessities in this category.

Physical Survival Needs

Biological vs Physical – Here is a breakthrough! My biological, which is what I am calling my body, is not me! My mind exists within my biological unit which is what everyone who knows me recognizes as me. However, who I am is in the neurocircuitry of my mind. Of course, ultimately, every sphere of consciousness is about physical survival.

My behavior is somewhat influenced by my biological in terms of my DNA predispositions as well as my hormone levels. Things such as my personality traits that are DNA driven, my brain chemistry type behavior traits that are inherited due to DNA, due to physical structure, physical chemical balances and other things like that. These are the non-consciously controlled aspects of my mind, but they ARE capable of being controlled BY my mind. So, my biological support system for my mind is just that and my mind is in conscious control of my biological unit. This includes the brain tissue where my mind resides just as in an AI, the software that is coding its actions is also residing in the hardware that is its equivalent of the biological unit which is the actual hardware. This is a very fascinating thing. Our conscious mind can actually control our instinctive DNA driven behaviors. It can do the same thing with our emotions and with the other aspects of our behavior that are not consciously derived, such as brain chemistry levels and so forth. Though I have to say that in some cases, such as in our serotonin levels, these are so fundamental to our mood that it takes an extreme amount of effort if it's not too challenging to be practical to manage one's conscious mind in contradiction to serotonin levels. This is because serotonin levels are so fundamental to mood and mood can have a powerful effect on conscious decision making.

Physical Survival

We would be remiss if we did not discuss the physical aspect of consciousness in HI. For without the body, the mind does not have a brain within which to function. So, the physical body is of paramount importance to the survival of the HI. Continuing, the different aspects of human physical fitness include being at our right weight, nutrition, and cardiovascular condition. They also include being in a suitable shape to do the things that we need to do to ensure physical survival including seeking shelter, self-defense both personal and military, being physically clean and attractive so that our social and political spheres are optimized.

My previous book titled "Eating Small" provides the weight management solution or coping skill. General fitness must be carefully approached as there are many examples of otherwise fit people who drop dead during overly vigorous sessions.

Energy

We need energy to power our physical consciousness residence – Human or Artificial. For HI it is food and drink. For AI it is electricity and in both intelligences, it is to power the host unit that the intelligence resides in. For HI it's our body and for AI it's the computer that the AI software resides in.

Air

For HI, oxygen is necessary for the survival of the brain of the host. For AI, air is not necessary.

Water

Same as air.

Temperature

HI host bodies are maintained at 98.6 degrees F and require an outside temperature that facilitates that 98.6 degree F internal temp. AI host equipment has a much larger temperature range but is also limited.

Injury (accidents included)

For HI, injuries to the host body can cause death or severe impairment and can also impair or render unusable the brain tissue itself resulting in the termination of consciousness. For AI, destruction of the hardware upon which the AI resides, results in the same thing for the resident AI, however, backup to an external storage that survives the destruction enables full recoverability of the AI itself.

Health

In HI, a loss of health resulting in death has the same result as death from injury. Other types of HI related health issues include brain disfunction from diseases that erode the memory capabilities of the brain, thus impairing the AI with like severity. Likewise, over time, HI brain efficiency can deteriorate from a lack of good health. This is not applicable for AI.

Fitness

In HI, fitness and health are quite significantly connected so same as health. This is not applicable for AI.

Weight Management

In HI, obesity can result in early death, obesity related diseases and organ impairment so this is undesirable. See my book "Eating Small". This is not applicable for AI.

Nutrition

In HI, nutritional deficiencies can impair brain function. This is not applicable for AI.

Illness

Same as health.

Aging and Death

In HI, the aging impact varies by individual, but death of the body is the end of consciousness. For AI, external storage of a backup of the AI gives 100% recoverability.

Instinctive Sphere

How does a baby kangaroo know at birth to climb into the pouch of its mother? How does an infant human know how to suck its mother's milk from her breast? It is obvious that there are skills and behaviors in living creatures that are not learned and not chemical. They appear to be what we call instinctive or what I like to call "in the DNA" or DNA behaviors. Again, think "nature vs nurture". I tend to think of these as including the basics for early survival that are clearly not learned from the senses nor from other sources of information, nor can they logically be considered to have been inferred in some fashion.

Motor or Muscular Sphere

As with the baby kangaroo climbing and the human infant sucking, some of this is DNA, but much of it is developed over time. Think of the infant learning to grasp a bottle with its own hands and later learning to stand and later, to walk. Clearly, the ability to perform the proper muscle control is learned and refined with time. Even an infant's ability to use its eyes to track a moving object is developed over time. These abilities are achieved through practiced effort and persistence.

Non-Verbal Perceptual Sphere

This includes the hair on the back of your neck standing up (danger, fight and flight) and also sensory awareness such as sight, sound, smell, taste and touch. It seems to be almost all DNA type awareness and coping. I am also including adrenaline states in this category. This sphere is almost all instinctual but at the same time developmental as its not fully functioning at birth. So maybe we think of it as DNA stuff that takes time to develop and fine tune. Sort of like learning to use our muscles to stand, walk, run, throw, talk and more. It is there at birth but not coordinated or fully developed. So, we learn to optimize our use, which is "coping", of our senses, muscles and other DNA gifts. These copings comprise part of our childhood development as we grow.

Language and Logic Based Spheres

The genius, Alan Turing gave us is a way to digitize algorithms. That was the beginning of computers when he put "if, then else" and similar logic statements into memory.

This relates to both human and artificial intelligence.

If you pursue a degree in robotics, this will help you to have the bigger picture. If you are delusional, this will help you to break down your reality to examine it more closely. Each new experience is debugging your perception of reality!

Let's look more closely at the language and logic-based spheres.

Self-Talk Sphere

In our minds, we talk with ourselves. This excludes non-verbal, perceptual, sensory awareness which is something different as we just covered above. We form words and there is structure to the thoughts, such as "I am typing" or "Wow" or "That was an interesting dream". Frequently this self-talk is about external events or observations, such as what we see, hear or feel. It also can take the form of self-perception like "I can do it" or "People like me". This can also be in the negative as we might also say to ourselves "I can't do it" or "I always have bad luck". The nuances of this self-talk have a lot of impact on our conscious decision making in our selection of coping strategies as our belief in the success of a specific coping strategy is part of the selection process for which coping strategy to implement to achieve a given objective and our self-talk has a lot to do with the strength of our belief in outcomes.

Here are some examples of the types of self-talk:

The **To-do list** asks "what's next". This self-talk acts as the manager of what is being worked on.

The **<u>assessor</u>** evaluates. This is probably one of the most important functions of our mind and I have not ruled out that it is a separate function, but it probably is just part of the decision-making function. It is vitally important to discernment, judgement, wisdom and just as important, the avoidance of delusion or incorrect conclusion. In general, the acceptance of fact is not 100% final but is an ongoing discovery process as we validate with our ongoing experiences and learning, our ongoing awareness. The assessor function can include the evaluation of threats, opportunities and the validity of conclusions in general.

It is the assessor that determines the impact of experiences, as well as to make them either an explanation point, underline, bold, 40pt type memory or insignificant and trivial. It is also the tool by which we evaluate experiences as being factual or illusion, truth or fiction, deception or real.

For example, in reference to certain key books such as self-help books, history books and other sources of information, the assessor evaluates the credibility of these sources. How the assessor of APOC, that is each of us, evaluates these sources determines much about many other spheres such as social, political and ideological spheres.

It is important to note that not all the assessor's indelible memory work, imprinting, is done consciously. Many indelible memories are not consciously made indelible, but they are so for reasons such as surprise, excitement, lack of frame-ability in our model of reality, traumatic emotional intensity, embarrassment, danger, PTSD and sensory-impactful events. The real source may be repetition in our minds.

The deceiver knows when we are displaying a behavior that is not our true selves, as in acting. Another example is the pleaser, or the server, which are more of a persona that we adopt.

The watcher or listener or taster or smeller or feeler (sensor - focused on sensory). This is not really self-talk.

The decision maker – The DM makes the decisions and is a part of the awake consciousness. The DM is apparently in charge of what we think about, what we do, where we go. In short, the DM is in charge of the using of the mind. When we are dreaming, maybe the DM goes to sleep. How does that work? How does the DM come active again when we wake up?

The connector – connects relevant input to other memories. This appears to be on during dreaming (ODD).

Creative imagination ODD

The algorithm initiator ODD partial

The rule follower – sergeant at arms

The rule breaker

Stream of consciousness

Recall ODD

Dreaming

Imagination

Sleep/Wakefulness

Reading silently

Sense of presence

True self SELF-talk when acting

Danger

Anger at others (Road Rage for ex)

Music playing in the mind from memory self-talk

Guilty conscience

Painful memory

Fear memory

Embarrassment memory

Weariness or fatigue feeling

In addition, our state of consciousness affects our behavior. Here are some examples:

Mood

Emotional state – On the subject of HI mapping to AI for emotions, there's not a lot of pass through as AI does not have emotions unless programmed to do so. However, in a call center environment, emotionally angry customers can be routed to a high empathy agent and played some very tranquil music while on hold. This has the effect of soothing the caller while routing him to an agent who is best skilled for handling an angry caller. This is using AI in the contact center.

Stress state

Mental business activity state

Body temp state

Pain state

Confidence state

Physical strength state

Fatigue state

Comfort state – Here are some examples of comfort: physical, mental, emotional, cleanliness, sweatiness, stickiness, grittiness, skin, muscle soreness or fatigue, sunburn, pain of any type

Trust of other person state (levels vary)

Family Sphere

Parental

Parental - Our parents are usually the first humans with which we come in contact.

When we talk about the family, obviously we have the topic of the parents, which can include foster parents, day care, or any other caregiver. As I have said before, the initial coping technique is crying, which enables the baby to be effective at getting the attention of the caregiver or parent who then tries to figure out what the problem is and then addresses it. This crying technique also has the downside of attracting unwanted attention such as from predators and this needs to be considered.

Sibling

Once we grow a bit and even as infants we begin to be exposed to our siblings and not just our parents. Families vary but it is not unusual for there to be subtle competition among siblings that shows itself in a variety of ways, including passive-aggressive and other competitive behaviors. These form the beginning of our social interaction.

Like a dog growling when sharing a bowl, bone or a ball with a fellow dog, people can behave similarly when there is a limited resource to compete for. Siblings are probably the first competition we experience as we "share" our parents and compete for them as a resource. This competition shows itself in many other social spheres such as business, economic, political and others.

Extended Family

Our extended family includes aunts and uncles and cousins. These extend our social interaction to more people further enabling our social coping skills.

Ethical Sphere

The ethical sphere is learned after we learn language and begins with training by observation and parenting and progresses throughout life as we are exposed to the many language and logic-based spheres. Ethics vary by culture and so can change as cultures change.

Ideology Sphere

This sphere is a place of extreme polarized contention. Probably more than any other social interaction except perhaps military, ideology has caused many millions of deaths, while providing hope for millions, if not billions. It is a sphere of unverifiable opinion and yet provides a basis for folks to believe in a deity, leading to a hopefully kinder, gentler humanity.

Ideology – This is a highly controversial, divisive topic as it touches on the most basic human need, survival. I'm not talking about survival of the body but survival of the mind. So, the mind itself searches for understanding about what it is, why it is, where it came from, how did the brain come to be, how did we become the way we are, how did the universe come into existence, what is the meaning of these things that we perceive in our lives, how do we explain the unexplainable? As the centuries have come and gone, we have come up with dozens of different explanations which vary by location, isolation and other aspects. Some have evolved progressively over time.

As they use words to describe what they believe, they reflect the culture and the language of the writer. The fact that they were written is noteworthy as this indicates, since writing is done with a purpose, that ideology content is written with a purpose. Perhaps, in addition to providing answers to the timeless questions of immortality, what we are and why we are here, they have goals like creating order, good behavior in the masses, establishing rules and behavioral code that the people should live by, with ideologies adding weight to the rules of man by stating them as being the rules of a deity.

All of this appears to me to coincide with the development of history, written knowledge. If you go back far enough the cave drawings are more about animals and hunting than deities. It appears to me that ideology came about the time of agriculture and the worship of nature or

Tengrism comes to mind. The drawings on the ancient Sumerian obelisks and Egyptian stones are more nature based. The sun, and other celestial objects are worshipped. As we did not understand science during these times, we were trying to explain, to create order out of what we saw, which appeared unexplainable at the time as it preceded science.

Now we know what a star is, what the sun is, etc. We have scientific understanding. The show was breathtaking to our ancestors. Comets, meteors, the sun, moon, planets and the stars themselves. All moving inexplicably and unfathomably overhead. We tried to understand it and explain it.

From a logical standpoint, one can say that these are manmade for the above reasons. We were trying to make a better world and it worked! We thrived and grew and made it to the present. I suspect much of it is trying to understand our reality, much as I am trying to do in this book. Since it is written with the knowledge of the day, our accuracy in perceiving the truth was limited by our tools and the science of the day. In short, we did the best we could at inferring a credible deduction about our reality that withstands the test of time. For example, the Egyptian ideology was incorrect in perceiving the sun as a deity, though its electromagnetic radiation energy gives life to plants and thereby us. A good and reasonable inference at the time, but inaccurate as we know now.

As I described there is a great deal of intolerance here. A whole lot of coping skills in this sphere has involved assimilation. Accepting the prevailing ideology of those in power. This has been necessary in many cases to avoid being killed by the intolerant ideological powers of the day. Countless examples of this exist in our history.

Social Sphere

Our social sphere is where we connect with other intelligences, other "I's". These can be living or machine intelligences. Frequently, social interaction can be uncomfortable or painful, however the benefits outweigh this cost. Consider for a moment your personal development over the course of your lifetime. How much of it has been acquired from social interaction? What about your coping skills? How much of your repertoire of coping strategies was acquired from social interaction? Everything except crying? Obviously, socialization is a profound source of our not only data type information but also including coping techniques and a great source of our social development to enhance future social interactions.

In short, socialization enhances our effectiveness at getting what we want by enabling us to increase our awareness, not only of information but also information about coping strategies, techniques for getting what we want.

When I was young, I read a book that dramatically changed my social life, How To Win Friends and Influence

People by Dale Carnegie. This book is highly recommended and is a good example of me learning from others, in this case, Dale Carnegie about how to improve my social skills. One of my biggest takeaways from this book was the chapter, Don't Criticize, Condemn or Complain. I carefully avoided doing these things and it was remarkably effective, though I had many occasions where I could have rightfully done all three. Now why was it effective to not criticize, condemn or complain? We think we are correct in our behavior and even when we know we are misbehaving, we deny it. So, external criticism just does not fit with that self-view. Call it delusion or dishonesty, but it is quite rare to meet someone who will accept criticism. In my experience it is best to do so one on one directly to the person, if you choose to do so. I find it best to be indirect about it and use questions always when I want to change people's thinking. In general, I accept people as they are and do not try to change them. Many things go into why people do what they do and think what they think. Its multi-layered and frequently goes back to their self-talk, their previous experiences and how they cope with reality.

Political Sphere

This is the realm of what is said and thought of us by others to others, in other words, what people are saying about us. This includes our image, our reputation, our public positions on all things and what is said of us in private.

Business Sphere

The business sphere is how we earn money or other assets that enable us to procure our needs in the market. It is characterized by all the good and bad of mankind as the resources are limited and competition is fierce. Coping skills are essential.

Business is a competitive arena and winning is important to the survival of a business. Second place pays zero. First place wins everything and so coming in second is a complete waste of resources, including time and money. It is better to not pursue a deal than to pursue it and lose it as the resources invested in a losing effort are better invested in a winning effort.

Faction Sphere

By faction I mean groups of intelligences that work together. This can mean two or more people on a playground, a political party, an activist group, a church, an ideology or any group. We should probably break these down by specific type as there are patterns to each that are unique. Frequently these cross other boundaries like economic and military in their impact upon our lives and so the interaction is complex. Therefor the coping mechanisms are also complex.

The issues are not always clear. Sometimes there is a lack of openness, hidden agendas and hidden strategies. The net effect of this is it is more difficult to ascertain what is going on, much less why it is happening. Secrecy is not unusual.

First thing is to understand what is going on. What is the membership and its extent? Why are they a group or what is their purpose? What is their platform, their agenda? What do they stand for? Only then can we determine what is our role in their existence. Then we can clearly identify an appropriate coping methodology. Is it affecting our economic, social, political, legal or some other sphere?

Military Sphere

I recently saw a video of a leopard sneaking up on and attacking a domesticated dog asleep on the front porch of an apartment. The leopard made the first strike on the back of the neck of the dog, super stealthy and snake-strike quick. This is a good example of the importance of awareness in the military sphere. The dog was domesticated and thought he was safe asleep on the porch of his owner's apartment but he was not. What you don't know can hurt or even kill you in this sphere and it is important to have warning, or awareness and to be prepared.

The sphere of external physical force is a crucial one to our physical safety and survival. This would include true military force as in an invading force from another country or tribe, as well as smaller groups all the way down to individual violence and intimidation. It includes gang force, riots and other civil disobedience. It does exist and it can end your life as it did for tens of millions in WWI, WWII and even on the streets of our cities today.

Legal Sphere

The legal sphere can cost us extreme money and time as we attempt to cope with it. Liability insurance can mitigate this risk to a large extent and is arguable a good idea in the modern litigious society.

Governmental Sphere

The periodicity of elections enables us to regularly affect governmental influence. However, governmental action can affect your life in the immediacy of right now. For example, legislation is passed on an ongoing basis that can impact your physical safety with weapons rights and foreign policy, your economic well-being with taxation, favor for various groups and property ownership. It can even affect your food supply as it has in Venezuela and other countries.

Economic Sphere

The depression of the 1930's had a significant effect on survival and more for decades.

Environmental Sphere

Pollution, chemicals, microbes and viruses are but a few examples of this directly affecting sphere and also includes air, water, and temperature. The plague of the 1400's wiped out 25% of the population of Europe. We currently have the CDC, the Center for Disease Control, a worldwide organization to mitigate this danger but it is not a perfect protection against disease.

Weather Sphere

Hurricanes, tornadoes, floods and other weather-related disasters do have a potentially deadly effect on our survival as well as other aspects of our existence, such as economic health.

Catastrophes Sphere

Volcanoes, meteor strikes, earthquakes, explosions, toxic releases and other naturally occurring and man-made, non-military catastrophes and accidents have wiped out the dinosaurs, whole cities and have the potential to eliminate life itself from the Earth. Coping strategies for these scenarios include avoiding areas around active volcanoes and earthquake areas as well as industrially dangerous areas. However, all eventualities cannot be completely addressed as a large enough meteor strike would eliminate all life on Earth. So, the only hope for mankind's survival is to have at least a survivable presence on another celestial object away from the catastrophe. As these have happened in Earth's past, catastrophes are a real danger to our survival. It is not a matter of if, but when and where they will occur as well as how severe they will be.

Now that we understand our DNA and decision-based mind, and the Spheres of Reality, we will address physical fitness in "AI - The Game of Consciousness – Book 2 – Eating Small". Then we will address how to get what we want in "AI - The Game of Consciousness – Book 3 – Effectiveness".

Visit us at ai-goc.com!

www.ingramcontent.com/pod-product-compliance
Lightning Source LLC
Chambersburg PA
CBHW031154250726
48655CB00002B/961